Your Path to Financial Fitness

Achieving Personal Finance Goals

Table of Contents

Chapter 1. Introduction

Welcome to your key to a financially fit lifestyle! Our Special Report naughtily titled "Your Path to Financial Fitness: Achieving Personal Finance Goals" is a treasure trove of enlightening strategies designed to provide you with the building blocks you need to attain financial freedom. We've done away with complicated jargon, infusing our tips with easy-to-understand language and practical steps that are enjoyable as they are effective. This guide will gently coax you into the wealth-conscious mindset you've been inching towards, and motivate you with the cheer of a trailblazer who dares to envision a more affluent future. As you dive into the must-read chapters, no matter your financial circumstance, you'll derive insights to pave your personal path towards meeting financial goals. Unearth this report; it's an investment in yourself that promises an excellent return, transforming the way you perceive and handle your financial health!

Chapter 2. Understanding Your Financial Landscape

The journey to financial fitness begins with an open-eyed understanding of one's current financial landscape. It's crucial to discern where you stand before you set your sights on where you wish to be. Let's embark on this exploration, probing into some of the fundamental elements that comprise your financial profile.

2.1. Evaluate your Income

The first part of understanding your financial landscape involves gauging your income. It's crucial to have a clear understanding of all the money that comes into your life, whether it's from a salaried job, a part-time gig, freelance work, your business, or investments.

To get started, list out all your income sources using '* Income' for each line as follows:

- Salary: $XX,XXX yearly

- Freelance work: $X,XXX yearly

- Rental Income: $X,XXX yearly

Rinse and repeat for each income source. It's important here to only consider consistent and reliable income sources. Do not count bonuses or one-time payments.

2.2. Understanding your Expenses

Once income has been accounted for, the next step involves decrypting your expenses. This will include obligatory costs like mortgage or rent payments, grocery bills, utilities, transportation, and insurance. Additionally, keep track of discretionary costs – the money you spend on non-essential items like travel, dining out, entertainment, hobbies or other luxuries.

Similar to the exercise above, list out all your recurring expenses in tidy asciidoc list format:

- Mortgage/Rent: $X,XXX monthly

- Groceries: $XXX monthly

- Utilities: $XXX monthly

- Transportation: $XXX monthly

Repeat the exercise for each recurring expense, then expand to discretionary expenses.

By organizing your income and expenses, you arm yourself with the knowledge of how much money comes in, what needs to go out, and what's left to save and invest.

2.3. Calculate your Net Worth

Your net worth gives a realistic representation of your financial health and is calculated as the difference between your assets (what you own) and your liabilities (what you owe).

Create asciidoc tables to list all your assets and liabilities as demonstrated:

Assets	Value
Real Estate	$XXX,XXX
Retirement Funds	$XXX,XXX
Other Investments	$XXX,XXX
Personal Possessions	$XXX,XXX
Checking and Savings Accounts	$XXX,XXX

Liabilities	Amount
Mortgage	$XXX,XXX
Student Loans	$XXX,XXX
Credit Card Debt	$XXX,XXX
Car Loans	$XXX,XXX
Other Loans/Debts	$XXX,XXX

After clearly listing your assets and liabilities, calculate your net worth. This gives a snapshot of where your finances stand.

2.4. Decipher your Financial Habits

After an analysis of your income, expenses, and net worth, it's time to examine your financial habits.

Do you fall into debt regularly? Do you save and invest consistently? Your financial habits are often driven by your mindset and beliefs about money. It's essential to know your patterns to change anything that doesn't serve your financial fitness.

2.5. Summary

Understanding your financial landscape is the pioneering step towards financial fitness. Consistent evaluation and management of your income, expenses, net worth, and habits constitute the foundation upon which wealth is built. With this understanding, you're well positioned to build a personal finance plan that aligns with your goals and lifestyle.

Keep in mind that success in personal finance doesn't always require profound changes or sacrifices. Often, the smallest adjustments in our financial routines can result in the most significant long-term impacts. Armed with the knowledge you've gained from exploring your financial landscape, you're on your way to a fitter, healthier financial future.

Chapter 3. Crafting a Personalized Budget

The heart of any financial fitness journey starts with crafting a personalized budget that not only serves as a financial mirror showing you where your money is going but also offers a comprehensive tool to steer your spending habits in the direction of intensified wealth and financial freedom. Understanding every facet of your budget gives you control over your monetary resources, and hence, is the ultimate empowerment tool. Let's take you through the meticulous process of creating a personalized budget tailored to your income, expenses, savings, and financial goals.

Let's start with deciphering your economic structure.

3.1. Unraveling Your Economic Structure

The first step in preparing a personalized budget is understanding what goes into your economic structure. Grab a pen, a piece of paper or your favorite budgeting app, and get ready to dive deep into your earnings and expenses.

3.1.1. Income Streams

List out all your income sources. Depending on the variety of your income, this could include:

- Regular Job
- Side Hustle
- Rental Income
- Investments

- Gifts/Inheritances

- Miscellaneous sources

Your main job's salary will likely be your primary income source. However, don't forget to include all the sources that contribute to your entire cash inflow.

What to do:

Action	Description
Document all streams	Carefully document all your income streams in a list.
Place amounts	Next to each source, jot down the amount you receive from that particular stream on a monthly basis.
Total up	Compute the total income you have by adding up all these individual amounts.

3.1.2. Expenses

Now, let's take a look at your expenses. They can be broadly categorized into two sections—'fixed' and 'variable'. Your aim here is to become fully aware of where your money is going. Some categories of expenses that can contribute include:

- Housing (Rent/Mortgage)

- Bills (Electricity, Water, Internet, Mobile)

- Food

- Transportation

- Insurance

- Health

- Entertainment

- Clothing

- Personal Care

- Miscellaneous

You should maintain transparency with yourself at this stage, as underselling or overlooking small expenses can lead to a misleading budget.

What to do:

Action	Description
Document all expenses	Maintain a detailed list of each expense, no matter how small it might seem.
Place amounts	Just like income, note down the average monthly cost for each expense.
Total up	Compute the total expenses by adding up all the amounts.

3.2. Creating Your Personalized Budget

Armed with clarity on your income and expenses, you can now move forward and create your budget.

3.2.1. Budget Breakdown

The most commonly suggested budget breakdown is the 50/30/20 rule. This rule suggests that you should allocate:

- 50% of your income to your needs

- 30% to your wants

- 20% to your savings and debt repayments

However, this is not a one-size-fits-all solution. You may have to tweak this depending on your specific circumstances and financial goals.

What to do:

Action	Description
Division of expenses	Classify your expenses into "Needs", "Wants", and "Savings & Debt Payments".
Allocation of income	Compare your breakdown with your actual income and expenses. Make necessary amendments.

3.3. Tracking and Reviewing Your Budget

Establishing a workable budget is only the first step; it is equally crucial to commit to tracking your expenses and consistently reviewing your budget.

3.3.1. Implementing Your Budget

You've created a personalized budget; congratulations! Now, it's time to implement it. Although it might be challenging at first, gradually it will turn into a habit.

What to do:

Action	Description
Expense Tracking	Ensure you track your expenses on a daily basis to ensure accurate data.
Reviewing and Adjusting	At the end of the month, review your budget and make necessary adjustments for the upcoming month.

3.4. Planning for the Future

The primary function of a budget isn't just to track and control expenses, but also to aid planning for future expenses and financial goals.

3.4.1. Savings, Investments, and Emergency Fund

Instant gratification often gets in the way of long-term financial fitness. Your budget should make room for allocations towards savings, investments, and building a robust emergency fund.

What to do:

Action	Description
Prioritize Savings	Make sure your budget allocates a portion of income towards savings.
Consider Investments	Build wealth by investing a portion of your income in profitable ventures.
Build an Emergency Fund	Maintain a buffer for unforeseen expenses to safeguard financial stability.

3.5. Designing a Lifestyle within Means

Living within your means is perhaps the most important yet overlooked aspects of budgeting. It doesn't mean sacrificing every luxury, it means balancing between your income and expenses.

Budgeting is an ongoing process that evolves with your lifestyle changes, financial goals, and needs. So, revisit it regularly and adjust as necessary. Remember, financial wellness is not a destination but a journey. Financial freedom has much less to do with how much money you earn, and much more to do with how you manage what you have. The right budget is your personal roadmap to financial fitness.

Chapter 4. The Art of Saving: Techniques and Tools

Saving is an art; it is the careful crafting of strategies that translate into financial health and freedom. Sit back, relax, and allow us to lead you through the dynamic world of different techniques and tools used to master the art of saving.

4.1. Building A Mindset for Saving

The first step to mastering the art of saving is developing the right mindset. Think of your income as a flowing river, with two primary channels – expenses and savings. Instead of focusing purely on what flows away (expenses), turn your attention to what can be stored (savings). Be mindful of your spending habits and audit them frequently. Question each purchase, asking why it is necessary and if it aligns with your financial targets.

Next, set short-term and long-term savings goals. These could range from small items like a new phone to larger ambitions like buying a house or a well-deserved retirement. Making savings goal-oriented will boost your motivation to put money aside.

4.2. Tools for Managing Your Money

Budgets are the most crucial tool for managing your money. A well-balanced budget is like a fitness plan for your finances, keeping your spending on track and ensuring your savings grow. There are numerous methods to budgeting:

- The 50/30/20 Rule: This method promotes spending 50% of your income on needs, 30% on wants, and saving the remaining 20%.

- Zero-Based Budgeting: Zero-based budgeting encourages you to allocate every dollar of your income towards some category, such as bills, entertainment, or savings.

Financial tracking apps, like Mint or PocketGuard, can be a big help to see your full financial situation in one place. Additionally, automatic transfer to savings accounts can contribute to a "set it and forget it" saving mentality.

4.3. Savings Accounts and Their Potential

Traditional savings accounts, high-yield savings accounts, and certificates of deposit (CDs) are standard tools for storing and growing wealth. They are insured up to $250,000 by the Federal Deposit Insurance Corporation (FDIC) or the National Credit Union Administration (NCUA), adding an extra layer of protection.

High-yield savings accounts provide higher interest rates than traditional savings accounts, allowing your money to work for you. Although CDs offer higher interest rates, they require you to lock your money away for a specified term.

4.4. Understanding Compound Interest

Albert Einstein famously said, "Compound interest is the eighth wonder of the world. He who understands it, earns it ... he who doesn't ... pays it." Compound interest can dramatically accelerate your wealth-building capability; it's interest on your interest.

By investing in interest-bearing accounts, your wealth grows exponentially over time. For instance, if you deposit $1,000 in a savings account with an annual interest rate of 3%, and you don't touch your money for five years, with compound interest, you will have approximately $1,159 at the end of the period - $159 more than your initial sum.

4.5. Debt Management

Part of saving is effective debt management. High-interest debt, if not handled properly, can cripple your ability to save. Prioritizing paying off higher-interest debt can free up your income to be put into savings.

Balance transfer credit cards with low or no interest for a specific time can help you manage your credit card debt. Also, student loan refinancing or personal loans can help in managing large lump sum debts.

4.6. Planning for Retirement

Retirement might seem far off, but it's never too early to plan. Employer-sponsored 401(k) plans or Individual Retirement Accounts (IRA) can provide a solid foundation for your retirement savings. They offer tax advantages and often employer matching for 401(k)s, leveraging added interest income towards your retirement goal.

4.7. Investing

An indirectly related but substantial method to increase savings is investing. Stocks, bonds, mutual funds, or real estate can provide substantial returns over time, despite inherent risks. Educate yourself first, as it's crucial to understand how investments work and the risk you're taking.

By assembling a diversified portfolio, you can balance risk while maximizing returns. Investing in low-cost index funds or exchange-traded funds (ETFs), for instance, spreads your risk across a broad market index.

4.8. Emergency Fund: Be Prepared

One of the most crucial savings goals is an emergency fund. It cushions you against unexpected expenses, such as a car repair or medical bill, without derailing your saving goals. The standard advice is to have three to six months' worth of living expenses saved in your emergency fund.

By honing your mastery of the tools and techniques discussed above, understand that the art of saving is ultimately personal – a reflection of goals, risks, timings, and a touch of divine thrift. It's never too soon nor too late to start practicing this interactive artform, which promises to secure a financially fit future for you.

Chapter 5. Investing 101: Making Your Money Work for You

It's no secret that generating and saving money is relatively more straightforward than investing it. But to navigate the road to financial fitness, it's essential to understand that money should function not merely as a tool for survival, but also as an instrument for wealth building.

5.1. Getting Started

Making your money work for you should begin with understanding your financial goals and timeframe. Are you saving for a holiday getaway, a new car, a down payment on a home, future children's college, or early retirement? Once you're clear on your goals, correlate them with appropriate investment strategies. Short-term goals can align with less volatile assets like saving bonds or certificates of deposit while long-term goals might align better with stocks or real estate.

Next, familiarize yourself with the four fundamental types of investments, also known as "asset classes": stocks (equities), bonds (fixed income), cash equivalents, and alternative investments like real estate, commodities, and cryptocurrencies.

5.2. Understanding Stocks and Bonds

In easy-to-understand terms, buying a stock is essentially purchasing a share of a company's future profit. Stocks can provide higher returns over time, but they also come with increased risk and volatility.

Bonds, on the other hand, are lending your money to a government or company in exchange for a fixed return over a specified period. While bonds typically offer lower returns than stocks, they are less volatile and hence considered safer.

5.3. The Scope of Mutual Funds & ETFs

For beginners, mutual funds and exchange-traded funds (ETFs) can be a great place to start. These investment vehicles pool money from multiple investors to invest in a diversified portfolio of stocks, bonds, or other assets. They offer the benefits of portfolio diversification a novice investor may not achieve alone.

5.4. Embracing Diversification and Dollar-Cost Averaging

"Diversification" is a risk management strategy that encourages spreading your investments over various asset classes to maintain balance and mitigate the risk of one asset's poor performance.

"Dollar-cost averaging" is a strategy for dampening the impact of market volatility by investing a fixed amount of money at regular intervals—regardless of the price of the investment. This approach allows you to accumulate more shares when prices are low, and fewer shares when prices are high.

5.5. Mastering the Art of Compounding

Albert Einstein famously called compound interest the "eighth wonder of the world." This phenomenon means that the interest you earn on your investments also earns interest, creating an exponential growth effect over time. The key to maximizing compound interest is to start investing as early as possible.

5.6. Setting the Stage with Budgeting and Saving

Ultimately, committing to a regular saving and budgeting plan is the cornerstone of strong financial habits. Remember, the key is consistency: regular, smaller investments over time can eventually build into considerable wealth. Try cutting out unnecessary expenses, automating your savings, and increasing your contribution as your income grows.

5.7. Investing Responsibly: Embracing ESG

Responsible investing, particularly Environmental, Social, and Governance (ESG) investing, has become increasingly prevalent. This approach factors in a company's impacts on the environment, society, and its governance practices during the investment decision-making process.

5.8. Understanding Taxes & Retirement Accounts

Investments are typically subject to capital gains tax. However, certain types of accounts, such as Individual Retirement Accounts (IRAs) and 401ks, offer tax advantages that are beneficial for long-term wealth-building. Always seek expert advice regarding taxes and your investments to optimize your returns.

The mysteries of investing can seem daunting initially. But with this foundational understanding, coupled with continuous learning and disciplined banking, rest assured that you're progressing surely and steadily on your journey toward financial fitness. May the wealth-conscious mindset lead you to an affluent future!

Chapter 6. Debt: Strategies for Reduction and Elimination

Understanding your current financial situation is the first step towards the journey of financial freedom. For many of us, 'debt' is a word that immediately raises stress levels, triggering images of insurmountable mountains of bills, notices and letters - but fear not, for this challenge is surmountable with determination and a clear strategy.

6.1. Evaluating Your Debt

To start with, it's important to have a clear understanding of your current debt situation. Make a list of all your outstanding debts, including credit cards, car loans, student loans, personal loans, etc. Your list should have these columns:

- Creditor's Name

- Total amount owed

- Minimum monthly payment

- Interest rate

This exercise reveals how much you owe in total and what obligations you must meet each month. It's a task that demands honesty but essential to confronting your financial reality. From this, you can prioritize your debts and create strategies to pay them off.

6.2. Prioritizing Your Debts

After recognizing all your liabilities, the next step is to prioritize them. This is crucial to structure your repayment plan. A common method is the 'avalanche' strategy, where you prioritize debts with the highest interest rates. By doing this, you minimize the amount of interest you pay over time. Another popular method is the 'snowball' method, where you pay off the smallest debts first to gain momentum. Choose the method that suits your psychological needs and financial situation best.

6.3. Creating a Budget

Creating a budget is your blueprint for financial health. It can be basic, tracking your income and expenses each month, or more detailed, adjusting for irregular expenses. There are several tools and apps available to help, find one that fits your needs.

- Income: Include all sources - salary, rent, dividends, etc.

- Expenses: Split between fixed (rent, utilities, loan payments) and variable (eating out, entertainment).

- Financial Goals: Short-term (emergency funds) and long-term (retirement, house).

The aim of budgeting is to ensure that you're not spending more than you earn, allowing for regular debt repayments.

6.4. Increasing Your Income

If, after budgeting, you find that your income isn't enough to cover your expenses with room for debt payments, consider ways to increase your income.

- Asking for a raise: If you've been demonstrating consistent performance, it may be time to discuss a raise with your employer.

- Freelance Work: Use your skills and spare time to take up

freelance projects.

- Sell Unused Items: Look around your house for items you don't use and can sell online.

Each little bit helps chip away at your overall debt.

6.5. Reducing Expenses

A quicker way to free up money for debt elimination is to reduce your expenses. Analyze your spending habits and eliminate non-essential expenses.

- Cut Down on Luxuries: Temporarily refrain from high-cost entertainment or lavish purchases.

- Downgrade: Toys and gadgets rarely define happiness. Evaluate each for its value and potential selling price.

- Review Subscriptions: Gym memberships, digital subscriptions, cable TV - Consider what you truly use and need.

6.6. Debt Consolidation

If you have multiple debts with high interest rates, one strategy is to consolidate them into a single loan with a lower interest rate. Remember, this strategy only works if the consolidated loan has a lower interest rate and helps you save money in the longer term.

6.7. Negotiating with Creditors

If your debt situation is severe, consider speaking to your creditors. Many are willing to work out a repayment plan, waive late fees or even reduce the amount owed if they believe that the alternative might be that they incur a complete loss.

6.8. Seeking Professional Help

If debt becomes overwhelming, don't be afraid to seek help. Many non-profit organizations offer debt counseling and can provide a roadmap for debt relief. Be wary of debt settlement companies that charge upfront fees and promise to reduce or eliminate your debts.

Remember, reducing and eliminating debt is not an overnight process, it requires discipline, patience, and resilience. It's about slow consistent progress - remember, the tortoise beat the hare! Make a commitment today to start this journey and see your financial health bloom. Debt is not a life sentence, with the right strategies and dedication, anyone can reach the summit of this mountain and come down the other side into the promise of debt-free living.

Chapter 7. Credit Score Decoded: Impact and Improvement

To many, credit score remains an obscure, abstract concept often tossed about in finance discussions. It's time to unpack this financial tool, elucidate its relevance and learn how to upgrade it to your advantage.

7.1. Understanding Your Credit Score

Your credit score, a numerical assessment of your creditworthiness, is primarily based on your credit reports. These reports compile data about your past and current debt, payment histories, and your use of credit. Ranging from 300 to 850 in most models, the higher the score, the better creditor you appear to lenders.

Credit scores are calculated using algorithms and models like the FICO or Vantage Score, with several key components affecting them: payment history, debt amount, length of credit history, credit mix, and new credit.

Payment History (35%): This is a record of your payments towards your debts, and is the most influential factor in your credit score. It checks whether you've paid your bills on time or have had any late or skipped payments.

Amounts Owed (30%): This refers to the total amount of debt you have, as well as your 'credit utilization rate'—the ratio of your outstanding balance compared to your overall credit limit. A lower utilization rate fosters a better score.

Length of Credit History (15%): This includes the age of your oldest credit account, your newest one and the average age of all your accounts.

Credit Mix (10%): This considers the various types of debt you owe, for instance, credit cards, home loans, car loans, educational loans, etc.

New Credit (10%): This relates to the recent credit accounts or loans you have taken. A large number of new accounts could indicate higher risk, potentially lowering your score.

7.2. Your Credit Score and Its Significance

Credit scores are a crucial element in the lending process. Lenders use them to determine whether or not to extend credit, the terms of the credit, and the interest rate. Landlords may review them to decide if you're a reliable tenant. Some employers might even check them before offering you a job.

For example, securing a mortgage requires a good credit score. Here, even a slight variation in your score could mean a considerable difference in your interest rate, which could amount to a notable sum over the life of your mortgage.

7.3. The Impact of a Poor Credit Score

A poor credit score has far-reaching consequences. It can mean denial of credit or high interest rates when you do secure it. It can also mean higher insurance premiums and even difficulties securing jobs or rental apartments. This is because a poor credit score can indicate risk, lack of financial responsibility, or circumstances indicating the possibility of default.

7.4. Improving Your Credit Score

The good news? Your credit score isn't static. It can, and should, be improved over time. Here are some strategies to better your credit score.

Pay Your Bills On Time: The simplest, most effective step towards a better credit score is to consistently pay your bills on time. Setting up automated payments can help avoid missed or late payments.

Reduce Your Debt: Work to reduce the amount of debt you owe. Start with high-interest debt first and strive to not just meet minimum payments, but to progressively pay more.

Don't Close Old Credit Cards: Long-standing accounts add age to your credit history, thus benefiting your score in the long run. Unless there's a compelling reason like high fees, maintain your old credit cards.

Limit Unnecessary Credit Inquiries: Every time you apply for a loan or credit card, a hard inquiry is made, potentially lowering your score. Be judicious about where and when you apply for new credit.

Consider Credit-Builder Loans or Secured Credit Cards: If you need to build credit from scratch or improve it, consider a credit-builder loan or a secured credit card.

Check Your Credit Reports Regularly and Dispute Errors: Since your score is based on your credit reports, ensure the reported information is accurate. If you find inaccuracies, dispute them immediately.

Managing and improving your credit score isn't a short-term goal. Consistent, responsible financial behavior over time will gradually enhance your score. And while the pursuit of a perfect score might appear daunting, every step towards better credit health puts you closer to financial fitness.

7.5. Monitoring Your Credit Score

Just like routine health check-ups, regular monitoring of your credit score is critical so you aren't blindsided by unexpected drops. Free annual credit reports are available from various sources. For more frequent tracking, consider services offered by credit card issuers or paid subscription services. It's important to protect this information, though: only share your details with trustworthy, secure platforms.

In conclusion, decoding your credit score empowers you to navigate the financial world with confidence, armed with knowledge about the impacts of various credit actions. Adhering to the aforementioned steps, you can improve your score and unlock doors to various financial opportunities. Let this understanding ignite a transformative journey to achieving personal finance goals and ultimately, to attain your financial freedom.

Chapter 8. Navigating Insurance: Protection for Your Wealth

Understanding insurance and its role in your wealth protection strategy is an essential step in achieving your financial fitness goals. This chapter will demystify the complexities of insurance, helping you decipher it as a safeguard for your treasures.

8.1. The Core Concept: What Exactly is Insurance?

Insurance is an agreement wherein an individual or entity receives financial protection or reimbursement against losses from an insurance company. The company pools clients' risks to make payments more affordable for the insured. Insurance policies are designed to provide coverage for various scenarios such as accidents, illnesses, property damage, and even professional liabilities. They act as a financial safety net, ensuring you or your assets are protected from unforeseen events affecting your financial health.

8.2. Types of Insurance: Which Do You Need?

There are several types of insurance, each designed to protect a specific area of your life or property.

1. **Life insurance** ensures that your dependents are financially secured in the event of your untimely death.

2. **Health insurance** covers medical costs associated with illnesses,

injuries, and preventive healthcare.

3. **Disability insurance** provides income if you become disabled and are unable to work.

4. **Auto insurance** covers damage to your car, damages you may cause to others, and medical costs of injuries.

5. **Homeowner's insurance** insures your home against damages and also covers its contents.

6. **Long-term care insurance** aids in the expenses of long-term care services beyond a predetermined period.

7. **Liability insurance** includes several forms of insurance that protect against claims of property damage or personal injury when you're at fault.

Your specific needs will determine which types of insurance are most appropriate.

8.3. Role of Insurance in Wealth Protection

Insurance serves as a protective shield for your earnings, investments, and assets. Should a crisis arise - an illness, disability, accident, or even your passing - the right insurance coverage can prevent your wealth from being exhausted. By strategically incorporating insurance into your financial plan, you maintain your wealth's resilience against potential setbacks.

Let's now delve deeper into the most common types of insurance.

8.4. Life Insurance: Safeguarding Your Loved Ones

Life insurance serves a dual purpose: it provides financial assistance to the family after the death of the policy owner and serves as a long-term investment.

There are two primary types of life insurance: term and permanent. Term life insurance offers a death benefit if the policyholder dies within a specified term, typically 10, 20, or 30 years. This type of policy is often less expensive and designed to replace lost income.

Permanent life insurance, which includes whole and universal life, covers the policyholder's entire lifetime. These policies also include a cash value component that grows over time.

8.5. Health Insurance: An Antidote for Health-Related Financial Stress

Health insurance not only helps to offset the high cost of healthcare but also ensures access to necessary medical attention and treatments. A solid health insurance plan can limit out-of-pocket expenses, protect from inflated medical costs, and even cover prescriptions, preventive care, and mental health services.

Depending on your situation, you might be eligible for employer-sponsored health coverage, public programs like Medicaid or Medicare, or individual market insurance.

8.6. Disability Insurance: Income Security for the Unexpected

Disability insurance stands as a bulwark against losing your income due to disability - one of the most significant barriers to wealth accumulation. It provides a percentage of your salary, usually between 50-70%, if you're unable to work due to an injury, accident, or illness.

Two types are typically offered: short-term disability (STD) and long-term disability (LTD). STD covers a portion of your paycheck for a short period, usually up to 6 months. LTD, however, kicks in after the STD ends and can last for a few years or until the disability ends.

8.7. Property Insurance: Protecting Your Assets

Comprising mainly homeowners and auto insurance, property insurance is a safety net for your most significant assets.

Homeowners insurance covers the structure of your home, personal belongings, liability for injuries on your property, and living expenses if your home becomes uninhabitable. In contrast, auto insurance protects you from financial loss in case of an accident. It's a contract between you and the insurance company; you agree to pay the premium, and the insurance company agrees to bear your losses as defined in your policy.

Understanding and utilizing insurance as a wealth protection strategy can retain your financial health, even under unpredictable circumstances. It's worth noting that insurance should be configured to your lifestyle, resources, and financial goals for optimal results.

By interpreting the nuances of different insurance types and integrating appropriate ones into your financial plan, you're taking significant steps towards safeguarding your wealth. After all, a financially fit individual knows that insurance is not a cost, but an investment into a secure financial future.

Chapter 9. Tax Planning: Understanding and Optimizing

The first step to effective tax planning lies in demystifying the jargon and intricacies that often surround the topic. In its simplest form, tax planning involves strategies aimed at efficiently managing your tax liabilities, so you can keep more of your hard-earned money. It's about understanding how taxes work and identifying opportunities within tax laws to reduce your tax burden. Optimizing your taxes is possible with proper planning, understanding, and legitimate methods.

9.1. Understanding Your Tax Bracket

Your tax bracket is the rate at which the last dollar you earned in a year will be taxed. It's set by the Internal Revenue Service (IRS) and varies based on your income. It is essential in tax planning because, knowing it can help you make strategic financial decisions throughout the year.

For example, if you are on the threshold of a higher tax bracket, it may be worthwhile to increase your tax deductions - either through increased expenses in case of business, more contributions to tax-deferred retirement accounts, or similar. This could effectively keep your income within a lower tax bracket, thus reducing your overall tax liability.

Proper understanding of tax brackets can also guide your financial decisions like when to sell investment assets. Understanding how capital gains can push you into a higher tax bracket can help you plan the timing of your sales strategically.

9.2. Types of Income and Their Tax Implications

Not all income is taxed the same way. Separate rules apply to standard earned income, dividends, long-term capital gains, and other forms of revenue. It is crucial, therefore, to understand the difference among these income types.

Earned income includes wages, salaries, bonuses, and other employee compensation. It's taxed at the standard rates set by the IRS for your tax bracket. However, the IRS allows for certain deductions against earned income.

Investment income refers to money earned from investments such as stocks, bonds, and real estate. It is further broken down into two main types: Interest and Dividends. Both are taxed differently. Understanding these differences can help you better structure your investments to take advantage of lower tax rates.

Capital gains are profits from the sale of an investment or property. They are primarily categorized as either short or long-term. Short-term capital gains (assets held less than a year) are taxed as regular income. However, long-term capital gains (assets held for more than a year) are taxed at a lower rate.

9.3. Deductions, Credits, and Exemptions

Deductions, credits, and exemptions, all play a crucial role in lowering your tax obligations. They are often overlooked, but using them can significantly impact your tax planning strategies.

Tax deductions reduce the amount of your taxable income. Examples of deductions include contributions to retirement accounts, certain business expenses, mortgage interest and property taxes, among others. It's important to keep track of potential deductions throughout the year since they can greatly reduce your tax liability.

Tax credits are subtracted directly from your tax bill. They offer a dollar-for-dollar reduction, making them more beneficial than deductions. Available credits include the American Opportunity Credit and Lifetime Learning Credit (for education expenses), Child Tax Credit, and more.

Exemptions used to be another method of reducing taxable income but they have been suspended for most taxpayers by the Tax Cuts and Jobs Act. However, tax exemptions for dependents, among other categories, are still valid.

9.4. Tax-Efficient Investing

Having a tax-efficient investment strategy can help optimize your taxes. This involves placing investments that generate certain types of earnings, in specific types of accounts, for tax benefits.

For instance, investments with higher taxable events (like corporate bonds or REITs) could be placed in tax-advantaged accounts like an IRA or 401(k). On the other hand, tax-efficient investments (like index funds) could be placed in taxable accounts. This strategy is commonly known as "asset location".

9.5. Retirement Planning and Taxes

Contributions to a traditional IRA or 401(k) are generally tax-deductible, reducing your current taxable income. However, withdrawals in retirement are taxed as normal income. A Roth IRA or Roth 401(k) operates a little differently – contributions are made with after-tax dollars, but both the contributions and earnings can be withdrawn tax-free in retirement. Therefore, making strategic decisions regarding retirement account types can lead to tax optimization.

9.6. Estate Planning

Estate planning involves developing strategies to transfer your assets efficiently after your death. Taxes can take a substantial bite out of the wealth you have accumulated unless you devise effective estate planning techniques. This could include trusts, gifting programs, insurance, and other methods to limit estate and inheritance taxes.

9.7. End-of-year Tax Planning

As the calendar year draws to a close, your tax planning efforts should come into sharp focus. Actions taken before year's end, such as making certain deductible expenses, selling off losing investments to offset capital gains, or making charitable contributions, can significantly reduce your tax liability.

In summary, tax planning isn't just an annual event but an ongoing process, and with proper understanding, strategizing, and timely actions, optimizing your taxes isn't as challenging as it might seem. Proper tax planning empowers you to keep more of your money, ensuring that you're in the best possible position to achieve your long-term personal finance goals.

Chapter 10. Planning for Retirement: Creating a Sustainable Future

Retirement; it's a reality that every one of us will have to face sooner or later. Whether you're just starting your career or you're at the peak of it, planning for a future where work won't be a necessity anymore is essential. Crafting a sustainable retirement plan ensures you'll continue to live the life you want, even when you're no longer earning a regular income.

10.1. Understanding the Need for A Retirement Plan

The rising cost of living coupled with growing longevity highlights the importance of securing finances for post-retirement life. A well-structured plan caters to your future personal and medical needs, ensuring comfort and peace upon retirement. It provides not just financial safety but also a sense of direction, empowering you to live on your terms.

10.2. Steps to Create a Retirement Plan

Crafting a retirement plan involves numerous components, including estimating expenses, considering potential sources of income, and understanding investment options. Below are essential steps to establish a well-rounded retirement plan.

1. Calculate your retirement expenses: Start by identifying your future costs, including housing, healthcare, traveling, and

hobbies. Assign a cost to each need and want so that you can come up with a reliable estimate.

2. Identify your sources of income: The next step is to assess potential income streams you can rely upon. It could be your savings, pension, investments, or part-time work.

3. Evaluate the gap: If your expected income falls short of anticipated expenses, you need to layout a strategy to make up the shortfall.

4. Decide your retirement age: Nowadays, retirement doesn't mean working until 65. If you manage your finances cleverly, early retirement is possible.

5. Diversify investments: Having a diverse investment portfolio is very important. Your investment strategy could include bonds, stocks, property investment, annuities among others.

6. Plan for unforeseen events: Life's unpredictability necessitates a contingency plan. Having a contingency fund earmarked for unexpected circumstances like serious illnesses is a smart move.

10.3. Understanding Investment Options

When it comes to investing for retirement, it's crucial to understand different types of investment options available. Here's a rundown of some popular investment options.

1. Bonds: Bonds are a safe bet, although their return may not beat inflation.

2. Stocks: Higher risks come with potentially higher returns.

3. Mutual Funds: A mix of stocks, bonds, and other securities, they spread the risk.

4. Real Estate: Property investment is a tangible asset that often

appreciates over time.

5. Annuities: A contract between you and an insurance company where the company promises to make periodic payments in the future.

10.4. Tweak Your Plan with Changing Times

A retirement plan isn't set in stone. It should be flexible enough to accommodate changing circumstances, such as new business ventures or unforeseen medical expenses. Regularly reviewing and updating your plan ensures that it remains aligned with your lifestyle and evolving needs.

10.5. Make The Most out of Government Programs

Many countries offer government-sponsored retirement schemes, like 401(k) or individual retirement accounts. These programs usually come with tax-saving benefits and are a valuable part of retirement planning. Speak with a financial advisor to make the most of these government services.

10.6. Work With a Financial Planner

Navigating the world of investing can be a daunting task, but a financial planner can help. They can guide you through different savings and investment strategies tailored to your unique circumstances.

Retirement planning is more than just about fiscal responsibility; it's about reaffirming the future we envision for ourselves. As you progress on your path to financial fitness, remember that the best preparation for tomorrow is to start today. Start crafting your retirement plan now, and rest assured knowing that a well-deserved and comfortable retirement awaits you ahead.

Chapter 11. Financial Freedom: A Road Map to Achieving Your Goals

The term 'financial freedom' is a broad term with varying definitions depending on who you ask. Regardless of the nuances in definition, one thing is common: anyone can achieve financial freedom by curating a financial lifestyle laden with good habits, smart decisions, and a sustainable approach. With the following guide, you'll have a roadmap to achieve your financial goals.

11.1. Understanding Financial Freedom

Financial freedom, in its simplest terms, refers to having enough savings, investment, and cash in hand to afford the lifestyle you desire without being tied down by financial obligations or constraints. It means you have the liberty to make decisions that aren't heavily influenced by monetary considerations.

Of course, this doesn't imply reckless spending or banishing the thought of work forevermore. Rather, it indicates having stable financial resources that ensure security for present necessities and future ambitions. To achieve this, you need not amass wealth like a tycoon; a well-planned and efficiently managed finance system is key.

11.2. Establish Your Financial Goals

Establishing financial goals is the first step on the road to financial freedom. Each person's financial goals are unique, defined by their ambitions, lifestyle, and financial commitment.

Identify your short-term, mid-term, and long-term financial goals. Short-term goals could include saving for a vacation, reducing credit card debt, or creating an emergency fund. Mid-term goals might include buying a home, paying off student loans, or saving for a wedding. Long-term goals typically consider retirement savings or a child's education fund.

Listing down these goals gives you a clear vision of where you need to be financially and helps strategize to meet these goals.

11.3. Plan Your Budget

Monitoring your income and expenses is essential to achieving financial freedom. It's not just about how much you earn; it's much more about how much you save and where you spend. A well-planned budget controls your cash flow direction and prevents you from overspending.

Identify and separate your needs from wants. Dedicate a portion of your income to fulfill needs, sparing a smaller proportion for wants. This balance ensures that you don't compromise your livelihood or happiness.

Remember, budgeting is not about restricting yourself - it's about understanding your spending patterns and controlling them in a way that benefits your financial health.

11.4. Judiciously Manage Debt

Debt can be a massive roadblock on your journey to financial freedom. However, not all debts are detrimental. There's a significant difference between good debt and bad debt. The former is an investment that generates long-term income or value, like student loans or home mortgages. The latter is what you incur when purchasing things you don't necessarily need and can't afford.

Crucially managing debt implies being in control of your repayment strategy, ensuring prompt payments, and avoiding unnecessary debt.

11.5. Investing Wisely

While saving is a good habit, it is not enough to achieve financial freedom. Investing wisely is crucial. It not only safeguards your money against inflation but also helps grow your wealth.

The stock market, mutual funds, real estate, startups or small businesses, and various other avenues are available for investment. Always do your thorough research, or consult with a financial advisor before making any substantial investment. Remember, every investment carries a level of risk. Strive to build a diversified investment portfolio to spread out potential risks.

11.6. Building an Emergency Fund

Life's unpredictability necessitates an emergency fund. This fund acts as a financial cushion, supporting you in unexpected crises such as sudden job loss, health emergencies, or urgent home repairs. It provides a sense of financial security and decreases dependency on credit during hardships.

Typically, your emergency fund should cover three to six months' worth of living expenses. Prioritize building an emergency fund before venturing into significant investments.

11.7. Review Your Financial Progress

Lastly, regularly review your progress towards your financial goals. Adjust goals as circumstances change, regularly assess your investment portfolio, and tweak your budget as financial needs evolve.

Financial freedom isn't achievable in a day; it's a gradual process that requires patience, dedication, and introspection. This review process offers an opportunity to acknowledge your financial successes and learn from your mistakes.

Step bravely onto the path of financial freedom, armed with the knowledge that the journey may be challenging, but the reward is a life unencumbered by financial worries. It is a trip that gradually transforms your relationship with money, allowing you to live a fulfilling life on your terms.